Arctic

Laura Pratt

Weigl

Published by Weigl Educational Publishers Limited
6325 10th Street SE
Calgary, Alberta, Canada T2H 2Z9

Website: www.weigl.com

Library and Archives Canada Cataloguing in Publication

Pratt, Laura, 1967-
        Arctic / Laura Pratt.
(Canadian ecozones)
Includes index.
Also available in electronic format.
ISBN 978-1-55388-631-0 (bound).--ISBN 978-1-55388-632-7 (pbk.)
        1. Natural history--Canada, Northern--Juvenile literature.
2. Ecology--Canada, Northern--Juvenile literature. 3. Occupations--
Canada, Northern--Juvenile literature. 4. Ecological zones--Canada,
Northern--Juvenile literature. 5. Canada, Northern--Juvenile literature.
I. Title. II. Series: Canadian ecozones

QH106.2.A7P73 2010   j577.09719   C2009-907295-5

Printed in the United States of America in North Mankato, Minnesota
1 2 3 4 5 6 7 8 9 0 14 13 12 11 10

072010
WEP230610

Project Coordinator
Heather Kissock

Designers
Warren Clark,
Janine Vangool

Photograph Credits
Weigl acknowledges Getty Images, All Canada Photos, and Alamy as image suppliers for this title.

Every reasonable effort has been made to trace ownership and to obtain permission to reprint copyright material. The publishers would be pleased to have any errors or omissions brought to their attention so that they may be corrected in subsequent printings.

We acknowledge the financial support of the Government of Canada through the Canada Book Fund for our publishing activities.

CONTENTS

Introduction 4

Arctic Locations 6

Canada's Ecozones 8

Arctic Features 10

Arctic Climate 12

Technology in the Arctic 14

Life in the Arctic 16

Arctic Plants.. 18

Arctic Mammals 20

Arctic Birds and Fish.. 22

Arctic Ecozones in Danger 24

Working in the Arctic.. 26

Eco Challenge 28

How Permanent is Permafrost?............................ 30

Further Research 31

Glossary/Index.. 32

Introduction

Canada is one of the largest countries in the world and also one of the most diverse. It spans nearly 10 million square kilometres, from the Pacific Ocean in the west to the Atlantic Ocean in the east. Canada's vast landscape features a wide range of geography. Yet, as diverse as the country's geography is, some areas still share common characteristics. These regions are called ecozones. Along with common geographic features, ecozones share similar climates and life forms, such as plants and animals.

Ecozones demonstrate the reliance between **organisms** and their environment. All organisms have unique survival needs. Some organisms thrive in cold, while others require hot climates. They rely on their environment to meet their needs. Just like a puzzle, every organism has its own place in an ecozone.

The Canadian Arctic stretches across an area of 3.5 million square kilometres.

Canada has both terrestrial, or land-based, and marine, or water-based, ecozones. The terrestrial ecozones can be grouped into five broad categories. These are Arctic, shields, plains, maritimes, and cordilleras.

In the Canadian Arctic, there are three land ecozones. These are the Arctic Cordillera, the Northern Arctic, and the Southern Arctic. While the physical environment of each ecozone is unique in its own way, they share the common characteristic of being extremely cold and far from areas of human civilization.

The Arctic is, literally, the top of the world. Much of the Arctic's surface water is in a permanent or near-permanent state of freezing. Meanwhile, much of its land is above the tree line. Here, environmental conditions are so harsh that trees cannot grow. Most of the soil in the Arctic is **permafrost**, or permanently frozen. As such, plants and animals that survive here have adapted to endure the harsh conditions.

FASCINATING FACTS

The Arctic has three of Canada's five marine ecozones. These ecozones are called the Arctic Basin, Arctic Archipelago, and Northwest Atlantic.

The word "Arctic" comes from the ancient Greek word "*Arktikós,*" which means "near the bear." The constellation called Ursa Major hangs above the North Pole in the Arctic. Ursa Major means "great bear."

Arctic Locations

The Arctic accounts for more than 40 percent of Canada's landmass. It spans Canada's three territories, the Yukon, the Northwest Territories, and Nunavut. The Arctic also touches on the northern tip of Quebec. Within this broad expanse of land are separate areas with their own unique characteristics.

Arctic Cordillera

The Arctic Cordillera extends along the northeastern part of Nunavut and touches the tip of Labrador. The word *cordillera* refers to mountains. Therefore, the defining feature of the Arctic Cordillera is its mountains. In fact, the Arctic Cordillera makes up Canada's second highest mountain chain and is the only major group of mountains in eastern Canada. The Arctic Cordillera ecozone contains many well-known Arctic islands, including Ellesmere and Baffin Islands. These islands are part of the Arctic Archipelago that stretches across much of the Far North.

Northern Arctic

The Northern Arctic ecozone includes the remaining islands in the Arctic Archipelago. The ecozone extends across the Far North regions of Nunavut and the Northwest Territories and also includes the Ungava Peninsula, on the northern tip of Quebec. Well-known islands in this ecozone include Prince of Wales, Victoria, and Somerset Islands. Iqaluit, the capital city of Nunavut, is also found in this ecozone.

Baffin Island is the largest island in Canada and the fifth largest island in the world.

Rankin Inlet is located on the west coast of Hudson Bay. It has a population of about 2,500.

Southern Arctic

The Southern Arctic ecozone stretches across the northern part of Canada's mainland. Beginning at the Alaska border, it crosses over the Yukon, Northwest Territories, Nunavut, and northern Quebec. Its southern border runs along the **tree line**. Inuit peoples account for most of the ecozone's population. Major communities in the ecozone include Tuktoyaktuk, Coppermine, and Rankin Inlet.

FASCINATING FACTS

Some of the rock formations in the Arctic are 65 million years old. In fact, geologists have found rocks in the Canadian Arctic that are more than four billion years old, which they believe were part of the very first continent on Earth.

The Challenger Mountains, located on Ellesmere Island, make up the world's northernmost mountain chain.

CANADA'S ECOZONES

Canada has five major ecozone categories. Like the Arctic, however, these categories can be broken down into specific ecozones. The inset map shows where these ecozones are located.

Look closely at the map of the Arctic ecozones. Besides their northerly location, what other features do the Arctic ecozones appear to have?

Pacific Maritime

Montane Cordillera

Boreal Cordillera

Taiga Cordillera

Taiga Plains

Boreal Plains

Hudson Plains

Prairie

Taiga Shield

Boreal Shield

Mixedwood Plains

Atlantic Maritime

Southern Arctic

Northern Arctic

Arctic Cordillera

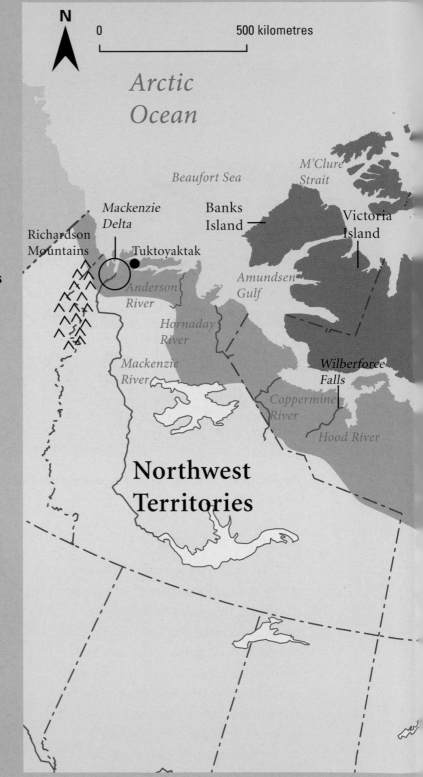

Axel
Heiber
Island

*Agassiz
Ice Cap*

*Bache
Peninsula*

Bathurst
Island

Ellesmere
Island

Prince of
Wales Island

Devon
Island

Bylot Island

Baffin Bay

GREENLAND

*Barnes
Ice Cap*

Somerset
Island

*Penny
Ice Cap*

Davis Strait

*Melville
Peninsula*

Cumberland Peninsula
Hoare Bay
Cumberland Sound

Nunavut

Baffin Island

● Iqaluit

Torngat
Mountains

*Ungava
Peninsula*

Labrador Sea

● Rankin Inlet

UNITED
STATES

Hudson Bay

Quebec

Labrador

Arctic Features

The Arctic is known mainly as an endless landscape of snow and ice. While this may be true to an extent, the Arctic and its ecozones are actually made up of a variety of physical features.

Hills and Mountains

Due to its nearness to the Arctic Cordillera, the eastern side of the northern Arctic ecozone features hilly terrain. Much of the land in this area is rocky, with exposed bedrock. The land often comes to an abrupt halt at the water's edge, and dramatic cliffs rise several hundred metres above the water's surface. The mountains of the Arctic Cordillera have their own dramatic effect. Rising more than 2,000 metres, their snow-capped peaks contrast greatly with the valleys and **fjords** that sit at their base.

The steep cliffs of Canada's Arctic coast are prime nesting areas for a variety of birds.

Plains and Plateaus

The landscape of the Arctic changes gradually from west to east. In the west, the land is made up mainly of rolling plains. There are two types of plains in the Arctic ecozones. The coastal plains are found in areas approaching Arctic waters. The interior plains are located deeper inland. The main features of the interior plains are drumlins, which are oblong mounds formed by glacier movement. Moving eastward, the plains gradually turn into plateaus. Plateaus are elevated plains. At one time, they may have been mountains, but they were **eroded** by **glacier** activity. The Brodeur and Borden Plateaus are two of the plateaus found in the northern Arctic ecozone.

Over time, glaciers such as those found on Nunavut's Axel Heiberg Island affect the geography of the land.

Eskers can be up to 100 metres wide and 50 metres high. Most eskers are only a few kilometres in length.

Icefields, Ice Caps, and Glaciers

Icefields, ice caps, and glaciers have much in common. All are large masses of ice that are in constant movement. Icefields and their larger form, ice caps, however, move outward in many directions while a glacier moves downward from elevated land. In Canada's Arctic, many icefields and ice caps are found in the northern part of the Arctic Cordillera. One of the largest ice caps in the region is the Penny Ice Cap, which extends across 6,000 square kilometres of land. Glaciers, on the other hand, extend downward from the mountains of the southern Arctic Cordillera. Sometimes, they extend from the top of the mountain all the way to the ocean.

Glacial Mementos

Glaciers have left a big mark on the Arctic landscape. The movement of their massive heft across the land leaves deep canyons and U-shaped valleys in their wake. Glacier movement also creates more unique landforms. Moraines are areas made up of the debris left from a melted glacier. This debris can include sand, gravel, and rocks. Kames are steep, odd-shaped mounds of sand and gravel that have been formed from the dirt left behind by a moving glacier. Eskers are ridges of gravel also left behind when a glacier moves. Some eskers in Canada's Arctic can be up to 100 kilometres long.

FASCINATING FACTS

Glaciers can be found on nine of the Arctic Islands. They occupy an area of more than 146,000 square kilometres.

Pingos are mounds of earth-covered ice. They can be found throughout the Arctic. However, more than 25 percent of the world's pingos are found near the Tuktoyuktuk Peninsula. Ibyuk, the second tallest pingo in the world, is 49 metres tall.

North of the tree line is a vegetation zone called tundra. The main feature of tundra is permafrost.

Arctic Climate

The Arctic's cold climate gives the area much of its character. The Arctic is large, so there is some variability in climate. However, long, cold winters and short, mild summers are typical across the region. Nearly every part of the Arctic spends stretches of time under a layer of snow and ice, and some parts are frozen all year round.

Arctic Cordillera

Temperatures in the Arctic cordillera never go far above 0 degrees Celsius. Summer highs tend to be only about 6 degrees Celsius. Winters are extremely cold, with mean temperatures of –35 degrees Celsius in the northern part of the ecozone and –25 degrees Celsius in the southern part. Even with the ecozone's proximity to the ocean, the climate is arid, or dry. Precipitation is minimal, averaging about 200 millimetres per year in the north and 600 millimetres per year in the south. Most of this precipitation occurs in the form of snow.

Northern Arctic

The Northern Arctic shares many climate traits with the Arctic Cordillera. The climate is cold and arid year-round as well. Summer temperatures can be a bit higher, sometimes reaching 10 degrees Celsius, but winter temperatures remain very cold, hovering around –35 degrees Celsius. This ecozone receives less precipitation than the Arctic Cordillera. It averages between 100 and 200 millimetres per year, with most of it coming down as snow. Snow normally covers the ground for 10 months of the year.

The *aurora borealis* is a natural light show that brightens northern summer nights. It is formed when excess energy from the Sun hits the atmosphere and is transformed into light.

The first frost of autumn turns the Arctic tundra into a riot of brilliant colour.

Southern Arctic

Summers in the Southern Arctic ecozone are short and cool, with temperatures only reaching about 10 degrees Celsius. Like the two other Arctic ecozones, winters are long and cold. In the northern part of the ecozone, the average winter temperature is −28 degrees Celsius. In the southern part of the ecozone, the average winter temperature hovers around −18 degrees Celsius. Little precipitation falls in this ecozone. The west receives about 250 millimetres per year, while the east receives about 500 millimetres.

FASCINATING FACTS

In summer at the North Pole, the Sun stays in the sky all day long. This is why the Arctic is called "The Land of the Midnight Sun." The Sun dips below the horizon by late September, and the days get shorter. By winter solstice, the North Pole falls into full darkness. It remains there throughout winter.

People living in the Arctic often try to block out the sunlight during the periods of 24-hour days. Sometimes, they line their windows with tinfoil so they can sleep in darkness at night.

The Northern Arctic ecozone is sometimes referred to as an Arctic desert due to its dry climate and lack of precipitation.

Technology in the Arctic

One of the greatest dangers Canada's Arctic ecozones face is global warming. Global warming occurs when **greenhouse gases** are trapped in Earth's atmosphere and create heat. This raises the temperature on the planet.

The coldest places on Earth are the first to experience the negative effects of global warming. It is important that the Canadian Arctic remain a barren, frozen place. Polar ice caps in northern Canada are under threat of melting if temperatures rise too much. If these ice caps melt, the oceans will rise, changing the land humans, plants, and animals inhabit.

Arctic sea ice usually begins melting in March and continues into September.

Canada's Arctic ecozones are an important place for scientists who study the effects of global warming. Scientists measure the climate, weather, and the rate at which glaciers and permafrost are melting. Scientists use weather stations, weather balloons, and ocean buoys to monitor Arctic temperatures. Weather stations record daily temperatures, storms, and other clues to help scientists measure activity in the Arctic ecozones. Weather balloons calculate gas levels in Earth's atmosphere. Ocean buoys measure the temperature of the surrounding water. They also measure water levels and can alert scientists if there are any changes. All three of these tools provide important information to scientists from some of the coldest and most dangerous parts of northern Canada.

Other scientists study the soil and surface of the Arctic ecozones. Scientists can analyze a soil sample to determine how fast glaciers are melting. They also use large drills to cut pieces of glaciers or layers of permafrost. From these drillings, they can tell how quickly glaciers are melting.

Some weather balloons carry instruments that measure wind speeds high in the air.

FASCINATING FACTS

Due to global warming, average Arctic summer temperatures have risen by about 1.2 degrees Celsius per decade since 1978. Some scientists predict winter temperatures in the region will rise by 5 to 10 degrees Celsius during the next century.

Scientists believe that global warming could eventually increase precipitation in the Arctic by as much as 25 percent.

Global warming may present the Arctic with opportunity. The rising temperatures could melt ice-clogged waterways, leading the way to more transportation routes and easier access. This could help industrial development in the area.

LIFE IN THE ARCTIC

A vast range of life takes shelter in the Canadian Arctic. Here, organisms experience some of the most extreme living conditions found anywhere on Earth. As a result, they have found many ways to adapt to living in this harsh environment.

AMPHIBIANS

Amphibians tend to be found in southern Canada, where they can obtain the standing water and rainfall they need to survive. As such, Canada's Arctic plays host to few of these organisms. Wood frogs have the most northerly range of any amphibian and are the only frogs found north of the Arctic Circle.

Wood frogs range in colour. They can be tan, brown, grey, blue-green, or red.

INVERTEBRATES

Invertebrates, or animals without a backbone, make up the most populous and diverse organisms of the Arctic. These tiniest creatures of the Arctic offer insight into how living things adapt to the extreme conditions found here. Many Arctic invertebrates enter a **dormant** state in the winter to survive the ice cover. Others cannot survive, but instead lay eggs that have a protective coating. This coating allows the eggs to withstand the freezing winter temperatures so that they can hatch the following spring.

MAMMALS

Many Arctic mammals have found ways to survive in the extreme temperatures. Some mammals, such as the polar bear, **hibernate** to save energy. Others, including the arctic fox, burrow, or dig, underground to protect themselves from the harsh climate. Still, other animals, such as the muskox, have thick fur or long coats that help keep their body warm.

The Arctic fox's coat is white in winter and brown in summer. These colours help the foxes blend in with their environment.

Lichens are often found growing on rocky surfaces.

PLANTS

In spite of its reputation for ice and snow, the Arctic is home to a variety of greenery. Like the animals around them, Arctic plants have adapted to this unique climate with its short growing period and frozen soil. The plants start growing earlier in the year, and they grow more quickly than plants in warmer climates. They do not grow tall because they do not have time and the soil is too hard for their roots to extend far into the ground. Some plants, such as mosses and lichens, stop growing when conditions become too extreme. They start growing again when the conditions improve.

BIRDS

The Canadian Arctic is home to both land and marine birds. Not all birds stay here year round, however. Most Arctic birds come to the Arctic to mate and lay eggs. They **migrate** when the weather turns severe. Since Arctic summers are short, birds breed and raise their young quickly. Many birds are fully grown and ready to face a brutal Arctic winter just weeks after hatching. Arctic birds are good at keeping warm. A thick layer of fine feathers, called down, traps heat.

An Arctic puffin can hold up to 10 small fish in its mouth.

Arctic Plants

Flowering Plants

At the height of the Arctic growing season, glorious meadows of wildflowers—including saxifrage, moss campion, wild crocus, Arctic poppies, and buttercups—spring into brief life. The most abundant growth happens in sheltered areas, where thawing soil has become moist. Most Arctic flowers grow near the ground and close together. This protects them from the wind and cold. Their roots grab shallow hold of ground that never entirely thaws. Some Arctic flowers have leaves that are specially designed to help the plant hold onto its moisture.

Dwarf willows often grow in clumps, forming a carpet on the ground.

Trees and Shrubs

As the Arctic ecozones are above the tree line, shrubs are more common than trees in the area. Some species of willow trees can be found in the Arctic. The dwarf willow, for example, is one of the few wood species in the Arctic ecozones. The willows lie flat to the ground, which protects them from harsh winds. Bearberry shrubs can also be found in parts of the Arctic. Bears eat the fruit of these low-growing shrubs.

Canada is home to more than 30 types of saxifrage.

Reindeer moss makes up about 60 percent of a caribou's winter diet.

Arctic Cotton

Arctic cotton, a type of grass that can grow up to 30 centimetres tall, sways in the cold Arctic breeze. These plants have puffy white cotton at their tips. People who live in the Arctic collect and use this cotton to insulate, or trap heat in, their clothing and boots.

Arctic cotton is often found growing in bogs and swamp areas.

Lichens

Lichens look like orange, red, green, black, grey, or white splotches on the ground. They come in a variety of shapes and sizes. Some lichens can grow up to 10 centimetres tall. Reindeer moss, one type of lichen, is an important source of food for caribou.

FASCINATING FACTS

Due to the short growing season, most Arctic plants are perennials. This means they lie dormant in the winter and bloom in the spring.

Scientists have discovered tree stumps on Axel Heiberg Island in Nunavut that are the remains of ancient dawn redwood and swamp cypress trees. These types of trees grow in much warmer climates. The stumps date back 45 million years, when Canada's High Arctic was as warm as Florida is today.

Plants prevent permafrost from melting. They protect the frozen ground from warmer temperatures and sunlight.

Arctic Mammals

Muskoxen

Muskoxen are generally found in the low-lying coastal regions, inland plains, and river valleys of the Arctic ecozones. Here, they can find ground-hugging shrubs for dinner. A muskox's long fur coat is its best defence against the extreme cold of the Arctic. The fur coat has two layers. The undercoat is made of soft, fleecy fur, which traps warmth to the muskox's body. The overcoat is made up of long, shaggy fur that reaches the ground. The fur is thicker in the winter months. When spring arrives, muskoxen shed some of their fur.

When under threat of attack, muskoxen huddle together facing outward. They charge at their attackers from this position.

An Arctic wolf pack can have up to 30 wolves. Most packs have fewer than 10 wolves.

Wolves

Where there is a herd of caribou, a pack of wolves is never far behind. A full-grown Arctic wolf stands 91 centimetres tall and weighs about 79 kilograms. Arctic wolves only kill what they can eat. Caribou is their main prey, but they will hunt other animals, including muskoxen. Arctic wolves store food in their stomach. They **regurgitate** the food to feed their young.

Caribou

Caribou belong to the deer family. They live in huge herds. Caribou migrate over long distances to avoid cold or look for food. A thick fur coat keeps the caribou warm. Each hair in the coat is hollow and traps warmth from the caribou's body to keep it from freezing.

Some caribou migrate more than 5,000 kilometres each year.

Polar Bears

Polar bears are easily recognized by their cream-coloured coats. They are the world's largest land carnivores, or meat-eating animals. Polar bears can weigh up to 450 kilograms. These animals have found special ways to stay warm in the frozen Arctic climate. Beneath their thick fur, polar bears have an 8-centimetre layer of fat, or blubber, that keeps them from becoming too cold.

FASCINATING FACTS

The Northwest Territories portion of the Southern Arctic ecozone is home to the world's largest concentration of free-roaming large mammals. One of these mammals is the barren-ground caribou, nicknamed the "buffalo of the tundra." These animals began their annual migration cycle through this area soon after the last Ice Age ended.

Muskoxen may look like bison, but they are actually related to goats.

Polar bears can smell prey as far away as 32 kilometres.

Arctic Birds and Fish

When hunting, a peregrine falcon can dive toward its prey at speeds up to 320 kilometres an hour.

Ground-Dwelling Birds

Ravens, owls, and ptarmigans are just a few of the ground-dwelling birds found in the Arctic ecozones. The ptarmigan is one of the few birds that lives in the Arctic year-round. About the size of a small chicken, the ptarmigan has a stout body, short tail and legs, and short, rounded wings. The ptarmigan is covered with feathers, even on its beak and feet. Foot feathers help the bird walk on top of soft snow. There are two species of falcon in the Canadian Arctic. They are the gyrfalcon and the peregrine falcon. The gyrfalcon is the largest type of falcon in the world. It preys on other birds, including the **endangered** peregrine falcon.

Marine Birds

Auks, murres, and puffins are among the many marine birds that live in the Arctic ecozones. Another marine bird, the Arctic tern, is known for the annual 19,000-kilometre journey it makes to the Antarctic and back. This is the longest migration of any bird. The Atlantic puffin makes its nest in large colonies along ocean shorelines. It is easily identified by its multicoloured bill and black-and-white plumage. The marine birds of the Arctic are remarkable for the way they have adapted to life at sea. Their toes are webbed, and their wings are short and stiff to move them through the water.

The thick-billed murre is a migratory bird that comes to the Arctic each year.

The Arctic char has the most northerly distribution of any freshwater fish.

Fish

The waters of the Arctic ecozones provide breeding grounds for about 130 fish species. However, few organisms can survive the icy temperatures of Arctic waters year round. Many **cold-blooded** organisms migrate to warmer climates when the weather becomes extremely cold. In Lake Hazen, the largest lake that is entirely north of the Arctic Circle, some Arctic char stay through the winter. Fish that do live in the Arctic permanently have adapted to cope with life in the cold. These fish swim more slowly than fish in warmer bodies of water. Some have a natural **antifreeze** in their blood to keep it from freezing. Many fish species retreat to the bottom of deep freshwater lakes as winter approaches to seek protection from the cold.

Waterfowl

In the warm summer months, the **wetlands** of the Arctic Archipelago attract many migratory waterfowl, such as snow geese, eiders, and red-throated loons. These birds use the wetlands as their breeding and nesting grounds. However, because the Arctic ecozones offer no trees for their nests, the birds must choose other locations, such as cliffs, boulder piles, and the ground.

FASCINATING FACTS

The thick-billed murre's short, stubby wings make flying long distances difficult. Instead, the thick-billed murre swims, using its short wings as propellers.

The boa dragonfish and the large-eye snaggletooth are two of the more unusually named fish in the Arctic. Both are deep-sea fish.

Arctic Ecozones in Danger

T the Canadian Arctic is a fragile environment. Global warming and increasing pollution are just two of the threats facing the Arctic ecozones. In fact, the pollution entering the Arctic is, in some cases, contributing directly to global warming.

In recent years, the Arctic ecozones have been found to hold many valuable natural resources, such as oil, natural gas, diamonds, and other minerals. In order to develop these industries properly, people and machinery have been brought into the area. Both create their own forms of pollution. Human-made pollutants are becoming an increasing problem as more human development occurs in the Arctic ecozones.

Heavy machinery is used to mine for diamonds in Canada's Arctic. These machines emit harmful gases while in operation.

Discarded oil barrels can leak toxins into the ground.

Pollutants, in the form of harmful chemicals, often rise into the atmosphere. Here, they are absorbed into water vapour and then fall as **acid rain**. The chemicals in the rain poison plants and animals. Some toxic chemicals present a problem because they stay in the environment for years.

Even radioactive substances have found their way to Canada's Arctic ecozones. **Radionuclides**, from the 1986 Chernobyl nuclear power plant explosion in the former Soviet Union, drifted into Canada's Arctic. Scientists believe these substances can cause cancer.

FASCINATING FACTS

Only slightly more than one percent of Earth's water is fresh water that is fit for human use. More than 70 percent of this water is locked in glaciers. Melting glaciers supply much of the world's water through lakes and rivers.

Oil spills threaten Arctic plants and animals. Large ships carrying oil to other countries sometimes collide with icebergs, spilling oil. Oil coats both water and the living creatures that use it.

WORKING IN THE ARCTIC

People who work in the Arctic ecozones are often involved in careers related to the environment or conservation of wildlife. As their "office" is in a setting unlike any other, people who work in the Arctic tend to be resilient and adventurous.

ENVIRONMENTAL CONSULTANT

- Duties: studying environments and determining ways to protect them

- Education: bachelor's degree in environmental design or natural resource management

- Interests: environment, nature, conservation

Environmental consultants study the ways in which pollution and human interaction cause harm to the environment. They find ways to protect the unique Arctic environment from dangers such as oil spills.

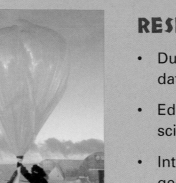

CLIMATOLOGIST

- Duties: analyzing and forecasting weather, and conducting research into processes and phenomena of weather, climate, and atmosphere

- Education: bachelor's, master's, or doctoral degree in meteorology

- Interests: physics, statistics, ecology, meteorology

Climatologists study climate in various parts of the world, including the Arctic ecozones. Much of their work involves analyzing patterns in weather and the changing temperatures of an area. Their study into weather is so specific that they can even estimate what temperatures and weather in general will be like years from now.

RESEARCH SCIENTISTS

- Duties: collecting and recording data in Arctic environments

- Education: bachelor of science degree

- Interests: Earth science, geology, biology

Research scientists study the plants, animals, and climates of the Arctic. They work with assistants to find ways to protect living creatures that call the Arctic home. For example, research scientists track the migration patterns of animals such as caribou and birds. They also study the effects of global warming on permafrost.

ECO CHALLENGE

1 What are the names of Canada's three Arctic terrestrial ecozones?

2 What is an archipelago?

3 How are ice caps and glaciers different from each other?

4 Why is the Arctic sometimes called "The Land of the Midnight Sun"?

5 Name three forms of technology used to monitor the Arctic climate.

6 What is the name of the only amphibian to be found north of the Arctic Circle?

7 How do plants prevent permafrost from melting?

8 Which animal is called the "buffalo of the tundra"?

9 How do thick-billed murres travel their migration route each year?

10 What are the two biggest dangers facing the Arctic ecozones?

HOW PERMANENT IS PERMAFROST?

Permafrost covers most of the ground in the Arctic ecozones. Permafrost stays permanently frozen unless heat or pressure is applied to it. You can demonstrate this principle using simple materials from the kitchen.

MATERIALS

- Large pan filled with water
- Five identical ceramic coffee cups with bottom rims that would make an indentation
- Hot tap water
- Ice water
- Small rocks (about 2 cups)
- Small sponge (for insulation)
- A freezer

1. Fill the pan with about 2.5 centimetres of water. Place it in the freezer. Place an empty coffee cup in the freezer, too.

2. When the water is frozen, remove the pan and cup from the freezer.

3. Place the cold, empty cup on the ice.

4. Fill another cup with ice water, and place it on the ice.

5. Fill a third cup with hot tap water, and place it on the ice. Be sure the cups do not touch one another.

6. Fill a fourth cup with heavy rocks, and place it on the ice.

7. Fill the fifth cup with hot tap water. Put the sponge on the ice, and place the cup on top of the sponge.

8. Put the pan with the five cups back into the freezer.

9. After 15 minutes, remove the pan from the freezer. Remove all five cups from the pan.

Feel the surface of the ice. Can you tell where all different cups once sat? Where was the empty cup? Where was the cup with hot water that sat directly on the ice? Where was the cup with the insulating sponge?

How will building houses, factories, and other structures impact the permafrost of the Arctic ecozones? What construction techniques could help protect the permafrost?

FURTHER RESEARCH

How can I find more information about ecozones, the Arctic, and animals?

- The Internet offers an abundance of information on all of these topics.

- Libraries have many interesting books about the Arctic and the organisms that make their home there.

- Many science centres feature data about the life forms found in Canada's Far North.

BOOKS

Banting, Erinn. *Tundras*. Weigl Publishers Inc., 2006.

De Medeiros, Michael. *The North*. Weigl Educational Publishers, 2006.

Kissock, Heather, and Leia Tait. *Plants and Animals of the North*. Weigl Educational Publishers Limited, 2010.

WEBSITES

Where can I learn more about the Arctic?

Canada's Arctic
http://polar.nrcan.gc.ca/arctic/index_e.php

Where can I learn about Arctic plants and animals?

WonderQuest
www.wonderquest.com/april-writer/ch8-plants-animals.htm

Where can I learn about climate change?

Cool Kids for a Cool Climate
www.coolkidsforacoolclimate.com

GLOSSARY

acid rain: air pollution produced when chemicals are incorporated into rain, snow, fog, or mist

antifreeze: a substance, often a liquid, that is mixed with another liquid to lower its freezing point

archipelago: a cluster of islands

cold-blooded: animals who control their body temperatures through external means

dormant: sleeplike

endangered: in danger of becoming extinct

eroded: worn away

fjords: long, narrow ocean inlets, surrounded by steep cliffs

glacier: a giant chunk of ice formed by snow that is compressed into solid ice over time

greenhouse gases: atmospheric gases that can reflect heat back to Earth

hibernate: to pass the winter in an inactive state

migrate: to move from one place to another with the seasons

organisms: living things

permafrost: land that has been frozen for two or more years

radionuclides: atoms with an unstable nucleus that give off radiation

regurgitate: spit up

solstice: the time at which the Sun is farthest from the equator

tree line: the point at which trees no longer grow

wetlands: land areas that are waterlogged for all or much of the year

INDEX

birds 10, 17, 22, 23, 27

climate 4, 12, 13, 15, 16, 17, 19, 21, 23, 27, 28, 31

fish 17, 22, 23

glaciers 10, 11, 15, 25, 28, 29
global warming 14, 15, 24, 27, 29

ice 9, 10, 11, 12, 13, 14, 15, 16, 17, 21, 28, 29, 30

mammals 16, 20, 21

North Pole 5, 13
Nunavut 6, 7, 9, 10, 19

permafrost 5, 11, 15, 19, 27, 29, 30
plants 4, 5, 14, 17, 18, 19, 25, 27, 29, 31
pollution 24, 26, 29

tree line 5, 7, 11, 18
tundra 11, 13, 21, 29